Morpho Aurora
water & wing

Britta Muldoon

BookLeaf Publishing

Presentation by *BookLeaf Publishing*

Web: www.bookleafpub.com

E-mail: info@bookleafpub.com

ISBN: 9789357445153

First edition 2022

ACKNOWLEDGEMENT

Thank you to my dear friend Meg Niesen for encouraging and cajoling me to finally write a book. Thank you Jordan DeSwarte and Hannah Gerber for your constant support and encouragement. Thank you Aaron Rose for helping me polish these poems and make the most out of them. . Thank you to Kallie Falandays at Tell Tell Poetry for helping me organize this book into a beautiful narrative arch that brought this book to life.

Thank you to the person who loved me for 9 years and was strong enough to let me go. The time we spent growing and walking alongside each other will always be precious to me.

Thank you to everyone of my family members, teachers, and loved ones who have been a part of my journey encouraging me to write with courage and honesty.

PREFACE

"Sometimes our ideas about love are really simplistic. We think of it as something that fixes everything, or, if the love is real, then you definitely have to stay.

The only way to really respect love is to respect its limits… you can love someone and still choose to say goodbye to them.

It's not necessarily a question of whether you love them, it's a question of whether they belong in your life."

- Tara Westover

First Responses to Error Proof Tests

Oh, Baby,
your daddy eats atom bombs,
catnip, and Camel 99s (*burning*),
likes only American blended whiskeys,
like his women:
one part schizo,
two parts maniac.

His favorite letter: X. Carved into
the whip of glass bottles he uses
to thrash his insides.
It's not enough until he breaks,
scatters—
sins leaking
from his inebriated eyes.
He counts his own fingers and toes
religiously like they were yours.
Like it can bring you back to him.

Baby, he's lost
in the dance of anarchy,
spun faster and faster
until half-truths
blur to lies (*burning*).

Keeps company with a public
that hides the same demons

in their empty pockets, barstools, and vials.
They remind him to
exorcise his ghosts daily
with their fist spit,
perforated punch-love and
waking up facedown choking on words they “didn’t mean.”

He told me, “She took the best shot and
it always felt like shit, burned
all the way down.”
It was only between dreams,
it was only passing out
and coming to that felt
like sleeping anymore.

My fingers were too gentle
when he begged me to pluck
his ribs—
guitar strings—
a lullaby for him to keep his fears at bay.
To keep your face (*burning*), Baby.

He tattooed your formless face behind his eyelids
memorized it by moonlight
inked in solid guilt.

I am sorry, Baby. I have no razor’s edge excuses
to explain him to you.
I don't know the map
of his hash marks on flesh,
forearm chalkboards.
He told me each mark
was an apology to you (*burning*).

An apology to
the nightmare sunrise
you would never see.

Still he keeps
whistling to your song, Baby,
by the light of the rerun reel
of a hungover horizon.

Every morning
he lifts your body from his bed.
Smile of Icarus wax
drifting far too close to the sun
or the edge of that roof (*burning*)
made of tortured family portraits).

Baby. Your sonogram seared into his palms (*burning*).
"We don't have time for Polaroids," he says (*burning*)
and lights another 99 (*burning*).

We Come from the Pit

We met when the earth was turning over;
fallen leaves and high hopes.
Surrounded by the musky smell of an earth surrendering
to the cycle of death and rebirth.

I remember how you used to look at me:
brief flickers of eyelids and down . . .
maybe worried if you stared too long, I would disappear
like the blue evening fog on Medicine Lake.

You smoked like you could light the world on fire
and dance freely on the ashes.
I wanted to burn the world to the ground with you:
my heart, the most beautiful arson we'd ever seen.

We were sparks flying upward against a gunmetal sky.
Dancing down the demons that made us fear love.
We danced till our feet fell in rhythm,
a trick that our bodies played on our minds.

When our legs were weary and the ashes of joy
burned low for the night, with shyness, I would come looking for you.
Finding you felt strange like knocking on the door of a place
I already knew was my home.

I remember the first time you held me:
we talked all night till our tongues were tired.
The cold of the early morning was creeping in
through the broken screen of your bedroom window.

I leaned in to tell you I was cold. "Can you hold me?" I asked,
my voice; quiet. I was worried that if I spoke too loudly
or too sure, the moment would fall and break
like a shot glass tumbling from your kitchen table.

Watching the sun rise through the landscape of broken blinds
and bare parking lots, I could feel your ribs press against me
when you would breathe. Exhaling, I felt the spirits
and blessings rustle, settling into my hair.

For a long moment, I could feel
the space between our souls growing thin.
Slowly, our hearts began to uncoil
themselves from years of hide-and-seek.

Quietly, we woke to sift through
the ashes of the night before.

This Is Not a Poem

A layer of white velvet obscured
the surface of the driveway.
So delicate and thin,
a snowy translucent veil.

The task of removal felt deceptively easy.
A cadence formed,
my body falling into the rhythm:
bend-scoop, bend-scoop, bend-scoop.

With each repetition
my limbs betrayed me.
Alone in my task,
ease quickly faded into exhaustion.

Bend-scoop,
your gaze—lost. Looking past me,
you were seeking a ghost shrouded in velvet.
Something you craved and feared in equal parts.

Bend-scoop,
cupping your face in my hands,
I did my best to bring your eyes back in focus.
For glorious moments, your eyes would find me and dance.

Bend-scoop,
each time you turned back toward the ghost
thirsty for water or velvet, I would lay my body down.
But even that could not stop you.

Perpetually exhausted
from the work of forging connection.
Trying desperately to change
my skin to the tender velveteen of your desire.

This alchemy was impossible
and I was pathological
in wanting to prove to you that I could satisfy
the drought on your tongue.

Each time, surrendering my body and contorting my soul,
I became convinced that this ache was a part of loving you.
How I wished you would reach for me in the same way.
When you could not, I would sing a familiar song to comfort myself.

The words went something like this:

Lower your expectations.
Do not ask for what others cannot give.
Do not ask for anything.
Make your desire smaller.

Make your desire so small no one can see it.
Make your desire so small it won't get in the way.
Make your desire so small no one can take it from you.
Make your desire so small that, when others disappoint you, they don't have to see.

Don't let them see how they keep drawing blood from old wounds.

Bend-scoop.

Take You

Make sure you split yourself into
one thousand pieces
so that everyone you meet
can take and take and take.

Slowly, without noticing it your voice
will gradually go dim.
Tuck your tongue under your teeth
and keep it only for yourself.

They will come for your tongue
when you least expect it.
Trying to tease it out of you
like the snake they believe you to be.

When you refuse to open your mouth,
their rage will spring; a switch blade at your throat.
The cold steel seeking to open you
and capture the last taste of who you are.

Fight it.

Bed

Make your bed and lie.

I will keep my shoes
and you keep your promises.
Take them out of my ears and
put them back into your pocket next to your cigarettes.

Let's not pretend you have
followed me for any particular reason.
You keep repeating, "What is it about you?
How do you do what you do to me?"

I have no answer for you. . . . Instead,
I gently graze your face with the tips of my fingers.
Maybe I can change your face
to something that resembles selflessness.

Something that would kiss me and tell me
not to call again for my own good. While you slept,
I thought of slogans for an ad campaign to motivate me to leave your arms.
Nothing persuasive came to mind.

My guilt wrote me love letters on the inside of my eyelids.

Afterthought

I am not sure you noticed my absence until
you heard the rust on the front latch (or your hand)
begging for touch.

I left
through the cracks
in your ceiling.

The water stains
by your closet are
reminding you to cry for me.

The splintered door
in your bedroom still opens
when you think of me.

You are still conjuring
the outline of my vulnerable silhouette,
cocooned in goose bumps and bedsheets.

I am blunt-edged nostalgia you continue
to stab yourself with even though
you are afraid of needles.

Western Union and the River

I saw you in my dreams
with eyes as dark and wild
as the midnight sky on the Mississippi.
You were looking for me,
pacing the shores of our memories
and digging in the sand for the footprints
I left behind weeks before.

You never noticed
how I slipped between your ribs years ago
and built a home close to your heart.
There is only hollowness now
in the place on your chest where
I used to rest my head and
I am miles downstream.

With your heart and hands buried in the sand,
you let the silt from this river collect between
your knuckles and your fears.
Each grain of sand deepens the cracks of doubt
in the foundations of all you thought
you could stand on.
I left.

I am not sure
if my absence was at
your choosing or my asking.
In any case, I washed ashore
on the dust-red Missouri soil.
Toes tipping on the Mississippi.

I am waiting.

Dear Sir. Stop.
Expecting your message in a bottle any day now. Stop.
Not sure if you knew. Stop.
I am gone.

Mornings

I miss you in the morning, when we would drag
our asses out of bed to make our way through the world in tandem.

Lying in the silence of the morning and I would listen
for your familiar sounds that told me what time it was.

7:30—the shush of the shower curtain
and the rattle of the faucet handle.

I would cook you a fried egg because I liked knowing
that you would greet your day with a tangible piece of my love.

I miss competing for the bathroom mirror
and using your razors in the shower.

I miss how you always forgot
to make a sandwich to bring to work.

But when you did it was always mayo on both sides,
yellow mustard on one, ham, three slices, and orange cheddar.

I miss your smell in the morning. There is a spot just behind
your ear at the base of your neck— it always smelled the strongest
there.

You smelled like the woods after rain,
of dark soil and damp leaves.

I miss how cranky you would be
before you ate in the morning.

I miss feeling safe being naked with all my parts
free and exposed in all their movement and glory.

I miss having a timekeeper.
I check my watch obsessively now.

You used to be able to tell time almost to the exact minute,
without ever having seen a clock that day.

I miss having someone to tell my secrets to.
I miss coming home to cook for you.

I miss how my hand fit in yours.
I could tuck my entire fist in your palm.

I miss the way my name sounded in your mouth.
I miss the myriad of nicknames you would call me.

There is a graveyard in my mind that I am building
to lay those words to rest. I miss feeling whole.

I miss how you would so generously volunteer
to be my makeshift bra while I was brushing my teeth.

Mornings now are so frighteningly devoid
of touch or sound or disturbance.

The soundtrack of my life
has become much quieter without you.

I fear how quiet it will become
with you so newly gone.

Seed

There is a silence that falls
when truth hits our hearts.
A space opens in us—
                    swells
                        & germinates.

Round and fragile,
putting down roots
to do its work.

Notes on the Apocalypse

When the break happens,
you will feel it in your body.
You will feel that moment of decision
fracture open in you
like the sound of the river ice cracking
on the Mississippi at the first sign of spring.

For a moment,
you will look at them from
across the chasm of the kitchen
and be tempted to fall back into their arms,
only to repeat this tired story over again—
a nightmare on loop.

Hear this—
if you go back now,
you will have to pack
every piece of your sanity back into a box
and watch it die slowly in the attic of your soul.

You will feel terrified
like a child lost in the woods,
even as you remember
that you have always been the only one
who can read the tender map of your heart.

You will wake to the hollowness of an empty bed
in the houses of your childhood
sheltered by well-meaning arms.

You will feel your guts rip open
every time you hear their name—
the sutures of your reality rupturing again, spewing
the innards of your pain everywhere when you least expect it.

You will spend time talking
to anyone that is safe enough
to hold your reality so delicately balanced
between well-adjusted human and a neurotic heaving mess.

You will dye your hair
and cut your hair.

You will begin to notice how good your body feels
when it is not beholden to the merry-go-round of someone else's life.

You will wake choking back a morning
without the long arms that used to enfold you,
sheltering you from the truth of the alarm,
signaling the expiration of rest.

You will get stoned in your car every night
and cry till your ribs feel like they will break
from the rattle of breath through your body.

You will call anyone who might be awake
because you need a witness as you watch
the house of your life burn to the ground
in your rearview mirror.

You will be haunted by words, phrases,
nicknames, songs, overused movie quotes,
and the smell of another body melting into yours.

You will be haunted by taste, by sound, by season.

You will want to scream all the time. (See also: cry)

You will want to scream every time you hear a Neil Young song,
every time you feel your playful nature rise inside you,
every time he calls you seeking a refuge
only to find a burnt-out shell
that has no roof or structure
that is safe for him to stand on.

You will do whatever you have to do to get through
this slow-motion slide through a meat grinder,
this tsunami of grief and love,
this long walk off a short cliff of all you dreamed
your life was going to be.

Dear Light Dear Energy

They tell you to believe in a God that is big,
but get angry when you believe in a God that is so big
that it breaks the walls of their neatly constructed theology.

What if you believe in a God that is so big that you begin to understand God as an energy and not a being?

What if you believe in a God so big that you stop making up carefully constructed reasons for excluding people from love and community?

What if you believe in a God so big that you begin to find truth everywhere and not just in the holy books you are told to read?

What if you believe in a God so big that you begin to see a divine spark in everything?

What if you believe in a God so big that you begin to understand that there is no religion or philosophy that can contain this energy?

What if you believe in a God so big that logic and science are not the enemy?

What if you believe in a God so big that you can't use the word God anymore?

Rosary of Lakes

These lakes have consoled me—
watery blessed oracles,
witnesses to all my unguarded moments.

Medicine Lake, Madonna of my high school secrets.
At your feet, I laid shame to rest on late-night drives,
collected pleasure from your swelling banks—
a slippery fish between my legs.

Lake Harriet, prophetess of love found and lost.
On your shoreline gardens, I opened my heart to forever
only to bury that same forever
in your soft sands with tears and curses.

Lake Superior, mercurial abbess of mercy and disaster.
In your surf, I've collected fear and awe—pebbles in my pocket.
I spent a childhood trying to build resurrection
from bleached bones of driftwood collected on your shores.

Lake Nebagamon—holy sister of slow moon's rising.
I planted my young feet in the dusky shallows
of my family history and built new sandcastle hopes
for the future, in a place that will always be home.

Lake of the Isles—sweet priestess of new beginnings.
I have pieced my broken body and tender mind
back together in the quiet of your rushes,
holding space for peace even in chaos.

My beloved devotees of constant change.

I pray to you, oh lakes—
that I may flow through this sorrow
with half of the dignity
with which you abide every season.

Oh, saints of waves and grace be with me.

She Knows

The earth knows our loneliness—
she stands solitary in the dark universe.

Perpetually close and yet far from all
the heavenly bodies that give her purpose.

The earth knows our helplessness
as she has no choice but surrender.

Lost in the tide between the sun and the moon.

For Disher

We trade secrets in how to survive
this natural disaster called life.

You lick me like a raw nerve ending
and I shudder.

I feel all the things that shouldn't make sense
when a stranger touches me—a fluency of body and ease of mind.

I fold into you like a wave over and over again, receding
and crashing back into your life with timidity and confusion.

I am an anemone. Brushing by me and I jolt
and flinch at the electricity that skips between my skin and yours.

Recoiling for a brief moment in uncertainty and
I feel my body begin to unfurl
as you wait patiently for me to find my heartbeat again.

This feels like a rising tide that is already out of control,
sucking us out to sea to survive on salt, sweat, and sun.

We are madmen,
castaways with a death wish called Love.

But we can't call this anything.
No one knows if this will all implode.

We will wake one morning hungover
and not believe a single thing that happened in our dreams.

Primordial Remnants

I arrive at your door dressed
in night air and looking for the calm of
I feel safe and uncomplicated—unburdened.
You offer some but not all of that.

Our relationship is a transaction of tenderness
and you graciously do not ask me about
all the things that make my life complicated right now,
pretending not to notice when my eyes tear up for no reason.

There is quiet exploration that enjoys
my body without pretense.
Moments of fascinated silence—
an astronomer of my birthmark constellations.
You offer the grace of sweet-tempered touch
to a body long used to settling for half as much.

It is I who cannot completely peel back the chain mail of my skin.

For those brief hours in your arms,
I understand a glimpse of what cherish could look like.

But my heart is not mine to give.
My heart is a caterpillar, an almost-butterfly.
I am a chrysalis.
I have been pummeled
by life into primordial remnants
with a delicate green armor.

One day, not soon,

I will open my papery wings and find a new world.

Ballad of the Pomegranate

How can I be thankful
for something that has
so leveled the house of my life?

I stand alone in the rubble of this
once intricate and grand home.

Before, the wind would rouse and wail,
shaking the house to the rafters
and I would insulate myself
with the fake comfort of these faultless walls.

I believed in every nail and floorboard.
I had faith in every door handle and windowpane,
even though I had to work
so hard to keep it standing.

I obsessively glued the house back together.
When glue did not work, I would shut the door
to whichever room I could not fix.
It was too easy to pretend
that certain rooms never existed.

Till in the end I was standing in a house
full of closed doors, convincing myself
that I was satisfied with the smallness of my existence.

The night before the house caved in,
I dreamt of you—
your strong hands

gently cradling a pomegranate.

Cupped so delicately at first,
open-palmed and free.
But that was not enough for you.

You craved the sweetness within—
greedy and impatient;
so you began to squeeze
and pull and dig into the skin.

At first the pomegranate
did not mind the careless bruising

because you had picked it, chosen it,
and you didn't mean to hurt it, after all.

Even so, one by one, slowly
you pressed each finger
through the delicate ruby peel.
You did not notice how your desire
for the most luscious parts of the pomegranate
were, in fact, destroying it.

All ten of your fingers—
starved soldiers that pried
at the skin revealing
its delicate white sponge so near beneath
the surface of its bright speckled exterior.

Ripping and ravenous,
you went back for more
as the juice began to run

down your hands,
snaking its way down your forearms,
dripping from your elbows.

The pomegranate did not understand
that it could not be enough,
that it did not matter because
you thirsted for sweetness wherever you could find it.

You needed each seed to be your own.
Crushing them one by one, dripping the
crimson liquid onto your tongue.
And the pomegranate did not protest
because it did not know how.

"I love you," you said. "I love you, I love you,
I love you, I love you."
you repeated over and over.

Though your prying hands were painful
as you slowly picked the pomegranate to pieces,
the pomegranate did not mind because at least
it knew that you craved it and longed for it,
even as you consumed it.

In the last moments before
I woke from the dream,
I saw you—
your hands stained
from the luscious liquid.
Your face was horrified.
Your gaze panicked.
The pomegranate lay at your feet—

sodden lumps of juicy red carnage.
your mouth and cheeks smudged deep pink
from your plunder.

"No," you sobbed. "Red, red, red! Please stop!"
You stared at your empty hands
and began to cry.

"I don't understand," I said in my dream.
"But isn't this what you wanted all along?"

I woke from the dream with a start,
my heart pounding
as if I had caught myself falling.

When I woke, the house around me
began to crumble.
The wind roared.
I could hear it prying every nail
and shingle from its place,
ripping my reality,
my safety, to pieces.

The photographs on the walls
began to fall and shatter.
The glass from the frames
looked curiously like shards of stars.

I sobbed and raced around,
trying to prop up every door
falling from their hinges.

It was no use. The foundation

was built on quicksand
and it thrashed and rumbled
and wrestled itself to the ground
as it collapsed into the sinkhole of my heart.

So here I stand, still and alone in this rubble.
As if the spark of our connection
hit the powder keg of our dysfunction—
pieces of my heart plastered everywhere,
bits clinging to bent nails
and fallen wainscoting.

You are nowhere to be found.

How can I be thankful for this?

And yet . . .

I might have lived my whole life
without daring to brave the open air
and step out into my own story.

So yes—thank you.

Thank you for forcing me to finally greet myself
alone in my truth—brazen, broken, and bare
with nothing left to shield me
from the brilliance of the sun.

Promises

I will not chase affection
like a rabid dog.

I will not thirst after
a well that is dry.

I will not place my heart on an altar
in front of you and plead with you to see it, to protect it.

I will not diminish myself, my reality
so I can fit inside yours.

I will not hunger after a heart that
can so cleverly dismiss mine.

It is not my job to keep inserting myself into your life
hoping for a connection that is not meant for me.

I will not make promises to myself or others
that I will not try my hardest to keep.

I will not keep promises to others
that damage my own heart.

I will not give more emotionally
to people who would consume me.

I will not tame my wild sexuality into captivity
to make anyone more comfortable.

I will value myself, my time, my energy,
my body, and my environment.

I will be sexy every damn day,
if I want to.

I deserve to take up as much
or as little space on this planet as I see fit.

I will protect myself from those
who would manipulate me.

I will not let others use this transcendent body
like a roadside truck stop where snacks and quick pleasure are taken.

I will give as much or as little of my body as I want
to those who touch me with grace, dignity, and honesty.

I will maintain my ability to act on my gut feelings
and treat my intuition as sacred.

I will give myself compassion when my taxed mind
and exhausted body need rest.

I will put one foot in front of the other
and keep walking this path because

I am fucking worth it.

Our Revolution

The first law of thermodynamics:
energy can neither be created nor destroyed;
it can only be transferred from one thing to another.

We can be consumed but never be destroyed.
We are a generation waiting for a revolution
that makes sense, waiting for plate tectonics to force
our bodies to recall the battle cry of the big bang.

It is here but we are just not listening.
We wait . . .
for something
. . . anything to unite us.
Maybe our revolution begins
with time,
a chain reaction,
an acknowledgement of the energy that surrounds us—
the energy that is us.

We are the constant resurrections pacing sidewalks in flesh.
Maybe revolution is not a fist or a plan.

Maybe revolution is your feet moving one in front of the other
and thanking the trillions of tiny deaths that made space for you to be.
Thanking the grain that is broken to feed us.
Thanking the plant that is maimed to clothe our naked frames.
Thanking the rain that gave up its place in the sky just to soothe our parched throats.

Maybe revolution is this:
Thank you.
Thank you.
Thank you.

For Murray

Putting all talk
of destinations aside,
having no map
does not mean you are lost.

Even if it's darker
than we remember in Bible stories,
does not mean you are blind.

Questions may seem closer
than the familiar voices of God.
Each one another dash mark
on an empty blackboard
as stars on a horizon.

You will write and find no words
as if praying to only paper,
mere whispers of firefly wings.

Your heart will keep beating
perpetually
like the sound of stilettos
in an empty hallway.

Prayers at times more like
suicide notes.
Love at times more like
dry heaving on truth you wish
you could swallow.

I promise grace is still hiding
there in the spacious silence
between your inhale and exhale.

I promise that life still
holds forgiveness between
mistakes and mistakes.

I promise you are not alone
between wanting to live
and wanting to die.

Monet

Dear Sweet Friend,
Sit with me and contemplate our life,
the sufferings and joys
that have wound around our tender heart.
It is up to us
to unravel these stories
so they do not choke our future.

Dear Sweet Self,
No one taught us how to love ourselves.
So much easier to make
bludgeons of our words.
So much easier to fashion whips and clubs
from the stories we repeat
to castigate us for everything we lack.
So much easier to embrace the continuing dark
than to look for the expanse of stars that live tucked just behind our bones.

You are a universe of glory in all its shy beauty.

When we tell ourselves the stories of our lives,
we trace threads of memories back and back to the points
where the pain of others confused our reality.

Though there is evil in pain,
the fault does not lie with us.
Let us open our chests—
crack open our sternums
and find that small infinite place to make a home.

Like an atom—
chaotic electrons moving expansively around a center—
we forget how spacious we are,
how boundless our beings were intended to be.

We settle for these small stories and very real pains,
threatening to convince us
the Monet of our lives is simply rough splotches of paint
that are all mess and no beauty.

Step back with me, friend, and marvel
at the light and shadow that make our lives.

For Mary Oliver

after "Wild Geese"

There is no need to measure yourself
on the human scales of impossible expectations.

There is no need to swim against the current,
desperate and broken-bodied,
only to crash yourself on the rocky altar
of someone else's judgement.

The only need you have
is to remember we are all adrift
belly-up on the surface of the universe—
limbs heavy and lax.
But we will not sink.

The only need you have
is to remember the ease of flowing:
breathing in and breathing out.

Regardless of our buoyed efforts,
the earth still spins around the sun.
The moon and unburdened stars
still float over our human atrocities and joys alike.

Regardless,
you are still here—
breathing in and breathing out.
Your breath the testimony proclaiming through your body:

I am here.

I belong.

www.ingramcontent.com/pod-product-compliance
Lightning Source LLC
Chambersburg PA
CBHW051742130826
49812CB00033B/964

* 9 7 8 9 3 5 7 4 4 5 1 5 3 *